May good luck be with you always!

Bonita Forsyth

SNOWBOARDING BUNNY'S

This book is dedicated to Jesse Forsyth for his love of mountain adventure.

MOUNTAIN ADVENTURE

Huckleberry Hollow Publishing

Presents
The fourth book in the Huckleberry Hollow Children's Book Series

Snowboarding Bunny's Mountain Adventure

Text and illustration by
Bonita Forsyth
Edited by Harold Rhenisch
Cover design by Jesse Forsyth
Scanning and interior design by
Jeff Kumagai, Ideas in Motion

Inquiries should be addressed to:
Huckleberry Hollow Publishing
C20 Forbes Rd., RR1, Lac la Hache, B.C.
Canada, VOK ITO

ISBN 0-9686275-4-4

Printed and bound in China

National Library of Canada Cataloguing in Publication Data

Forsyth, Bonita
Snowboarding Bunny's Mountain Adventure / text and illustrations by Bonita Forsyth.
(Huckleberry Hollow Children's Book Series ;2)
ISBN 0-9686275-4-4

1. Title. II. Series

PS8561.0697S663 2004 jC813'.54 C2004-902998-3

From the silence of the snowcapped mountains
unfolds a most unusual story
about the adventurous boy Jonathan
and the daring, determined snowshoe hare, Sunny.

They met quite by accident one bright afternoon
on the slopes of a small ski hill.
Together, on a single snowboard,
they cruised down the mountain and into a friendship
that lasted well beyond that fateful winter!
Now, four years later...

Even before the snow
Began to swirl and fall,
The distant mountains loomed,
Cold, white and tall.

They looked so inviting
To Sunny and John,
By the time the lake froze
Boy and bunny had gone!

helmets
avalanche beacon
probes
folding shovels
snowshoes
first aid kit
food + water
maps
compass
AVALANCHE
DANGER
FORCAST
LOW
www.avalanche.ca

They planned with care!
They were well aware
Of the mountain dangers
That were lurking there.

They studied the maps,
Knew the gear to wear,
Prepared for the worst
That could happen out there!

Why does snow slide?
When is it safe to ride?

The pros all know
When it's safe to go
Out there,
Hunting big air!

At the crack of dawn
The friends rode in tandem,
John on the snowmobile,
Sunny right behind him.

They blazed through the powder,
Cruised the mountain trails,
Skimmed a frozen pond,
Shooting out dragon tails!

When it started to get dark,
They parked the machine.
For safety, they waited
For the rest of their team.

Sunny's big feet
Help him walk on snow,
But Lee and Lindsey need snowshoes
To get where they want to go.

They set up the tents
Under a starlit sky;
Lit a bright cozy fire
To keep their snowboard boots dry.

They made hot chocolate,
Roasted dinner on sticks,
In the warm firelight
They dreamed of wild snowboard tricks,

While the northern lights sparkled
In the moonlit sky.
They all fell asleep
To the lone wolf's cry.

Next morning John and Sunny
Found the perfect slope.
They unloaded shovels,
snowboards and rope,

Sliced a piece
Right out of the snow,
And studied the layers.
Would it be safe to go?

YES!

We're able!
The snow is stable!
It's safe to go!
Everything we know
We learned from a pro!

The pros all know
When it's safe to go
Out there,
Hunting big air!

They strapped on their snowboards,
Cinched helmets up tight,
Checked avalanche beacons
And slid out of sight.

Sunny jumped first.
He sailed through the skies.
His friends down below
Could not believe their eyes!

They were not the only ones
Watching the daring hare!
From a hidden snowy den,
In a white and sunlit glen,

A fox sat drooling
Over the fat, frisky bunny
That would satisfy
His hungry, rumbling tummy!

At the same time Sunny jumped,
The fox jumped too,
Breaking off a lump of snow
As he tumbled through!

Sunny touched down like a feather.
The fox dropped onto the hare,
And that mighty lump of snow
Fell over the tangled pair!

It was all too much
For the slope of the snow!
The hill went sliding downward.
They began to roll.

Faster and faster,
They tumbled and they slid!
All the animals nearby
Quickly ran away and hid.

As Sunny was jumbled
In the thunder of the snow,
His snowboard dragged him under,
With a shudder and a groan!

He remembered his lessons,
Put his paws up by his face
So he'd have some air to breathe
In that little tiny space!

When the snow stopped moving
All was quiet and still.
There was no sign of Sunny!
John ran towards the hill,

Using his avalanche beacon
To guide the way
Over the broken slope
To where he thought Sunny lay!

Grasping his probing stick
In steady mittened hands,
He gently pierced the snow
To find his missing friend!

He felt something soft,
So he shoveled with great care.
It could be Sunny Bunny
Buried under there!

John uncovered Sunny's pack,
His snowboard, too,
And there lay the crumpled bunny,
Bruised black and blue!

His ears were bent,
His whiskers all askew,
And his leg was broken,
But John knew what to do.

He lashed that broken leg
To a long straight branch
And carried the aching bunny
Quickly back to camp.

John radioed his friends
To go for a helicopter!
"Come back right away,
Sunny needs a doctor!"

John dug a snow cave
And lowered the tent inside
To keep Sunny warm
And make a place to hide.

In the spreading darkness,
The fox, still looking for his prize,
Was sniffing bunny tracks
Under stormy winter skies!

As the wind began to howl
John knew no help could come.
He melted snow for Sunny,
And waited for the dawn.

In the blackest hours of darkness
The fox saw the lantern's glow,
Casting bunny shadows
Across the drifted snow.

Oh, no!

As the golden light of dawn
Just began to show...

Lee saw him from the chopper,
The fox was tearing at the tent!
The chopper landed with a clatter
That sent him whimpering to his den.

Sunny realized that evening
As the fire danced with light,
"Good Luck" had helped them to survive
From the fox and snow that night.

"Good Luck" and careful planning
Kept them safe on the mountain trail.
Now they're back from their adventure
To share this snowboard tale.

STAYING ALIVE
BACKCOUNTRY SNOWBOARDING

Forever they'll be dreaming...

Out there!

Somewhere!

Hunting big air!

The End.

Special thanks to Evan Manners
and the Canadian Avalanche Association
for providing valuable information on safety
in the backcountry.